Dedication

To Jenny (I sometimes feel you here, helping her along). To my family, I am so lucky to be part of you. To Al, loving husband and daddy, it's been wonderful seeing us muddle along and grow into loving parents. To Little Mabel for bringing Big love, joy and laughter into our lives.

Introduction

On this occasion I have stepped away from bag making to play dressing-up with my daughter. In creating these patterns I have realized a mother's dream come true: to design clothes for her baby and have her as the cover girl. Wow!

As a sewing-fiend mum, my desire to sew clothes for my baby is (unsurprisingly) strong. But finding the time to sew has been (unsurprisingly) tricky. As a mum I know how short on crafting time we are. We'd like to make unique and well-made clothes (quickly) and we have to accept that our little ones grow fast. With this in mind I have created cool designs that are quick to make and do not require yards of fabric. I know how busy you are and I know how much you want to make her something cute to wear. Because our poppets come in all shapes and sizes, various design features, such as straps, garment length and so on, can be easily customized. Where applicable I have given instructions on how to lengthen and widen (or vice versa). Measurements are given in metric (centimetres), with imperial (inches) in brackets – so you can choose one system and stick with it throughout.

You'll find that the clothes are beginner friendly but I have included sweet design details to make the clothes look anything but basic. I wanted my clothes to be easy to make, simple to put on, and finished to a standard good enough to handed down through the family. In short, I have tried to balance our need to be practical with our desire to dress her in sew-it-yourself fabulousness!

I think for many of us part of the joy of crafting is sharing and making lasting memories. So when you sew for someone you care about you give them love in every stitch. I created these clothes with a mother's love for her baby; I really hope you enjoy making and gifting them as much as I did.

Pop in and say hello here:

Facebook: www.facebook.com/UHandbag

Blog: u-handbag.typepad.com/

Love Lisa X

Basic Tools

1. **Rotary cutter** – this greatly increases the speed and accuracy of fabric cutting. Great for speedy cutting of straight fabrics strips.
2. **Cutting mat** – for use with a rotary cutter. Choose one with inch and centimetre gridlines. Some mats also have 45-degree angle lines, to help cut fabrics on the bias.
3. **Quilter's ruler** – these come in all shapes and sizes and are essential for use with rotary cutters.
4. **Dressmaking scissors** – choose scissors that cut all the way through to the tip, are as heavy as is comfortable (weight aids cutting stability) and are angled with the handles raised upwards.
5. **Fine scissors** – small and fine-pointed scissors are essential for precision snipping. Some have curved tips that make them brilliant for trimming seams neatly.
6. **Seam ripper** – not just for unpicking seams, a seam ripper is perfect for making incisions for buttonholes. Always replace dull rippers as they can do a lot of damage to your work (from slipping accidents).
7. **Disappearing marker** – these markers are my favourite type because they are more precise than chalk. Make your marks as desired and they will disappear within 48 hours – so handy! Always test before use.
8. **Hera marker** – this marker makes indents in your fabric from pressure only, so is perfect if your fabric is unsuitable for disappearing markers. They are also great for pre-creasing fabric for when you need to make folds. You could also use a bone folder.
9. **Tape measure** – to make measurement conversions a cinch choose a tape measure with metric and imperial measurements printed on the same side.
10. **Sewing pins** – I love flower flathead pins because they're pretty and easy to see.
11. **Sewing clips** – when sewing pins are unsuitable use these clips to temporarily hold fabric pieces together. They do not distort your work, as pins can, so they aid smoother sewing. I like to use clips when sewing with binding.
12. **Iron** – while this is not my favourite job, ironing is an essential part of sewing. As my sewing space is rather limited I use a travel steam iron and mini ironing board.
13. **Thread** – to make life easy for yourself (and to make long-lasting clothes) use good quality all-purpose polyester thread. Quality thread is easier to sew with and lasts much longer.
14. **Tailor's awl** – so useful for poking out corners (when turning out) or guiding your work smoothly under the machine foot (to help the feed dogs grab the fabric). They make sewing with gathers so much easier.
15. **Bodkin** – this is used for speedy threading of cord or elastic through fabric tubes or casing.

Also:

Hand sewing needle – there are times when hand sewing is unavoidable, such as when the machine can't reach the areas you need to stitch or when you need to sew on buttons.

Halter-Top

Perfect for play dates, happy holidays or running around at home, the Happiness Halter-Top is fun to piece together and super-quick to make. Why not team it up with jeans and pumps for a sweet, yet streetwise look?

Sewing Notes

1. **Seam allowance:** 1cm (⅜in) unless otherwise stated. Seam allowance is included in the pattern pieces.
2. **Pattern pieces:** the halter-top is made from: 2 x paper pattern pieces. There are 7 x fabric pattern pieces in total (including those from 'Also Cut').
3. **Fabric recommendations:** lightweight cotton, tana lawn, quilt-weight cotton, chambray fabric.
4. **Trims and binding:** cut all straps, trims and binding on the fabric bias.
5. **Strap fabric length:** The strap length is dependent on the age of your poppet. To prevent choking, straps for toddlers should be kept short. Straps long enough to tie a double knot will be sufficient (I suggest 40cm/15½in). For older girls, straps can be made longer for tying a bow (I suggest 55cm/21⅝in). The strap fabric height needs to be 6cm (2⅜in).
6. **Neckline binding:** cut the neckline binding fabric according to size – for all sizes binding height needs to be 5cm (2in): age 2 = 20cm (7⅞in); age 3 = 21cm (8¼in); age 4 = 22cm (8¾in); age 5 = 23cm (9in); age 6 = 24cm (9½in).
7. **Neckline elastic:** cut the neckline elastic according to size – for all sizes elastic height needs to be 6mm (¼in). Feel free to lengthen (but do not shorten): age 2 = 17cm (6¾in); age 3 = 18cm (7⅛in); age 4 = 19cm (7½in); age 5 = 20cm (7⅞in); age 6 = 21cm (8¼in).
8. **Back elastic:** cut the back elastic according to size – for all sizes elastic height needs to be 6mm (¼in). Feel free to lengthen or shorten the elastic length as desired: age 2 = 23cm (9in); age 3 = 24.5cm (9⅝in); age 4 = 26cm (10¼in); age 5 = 27cm (10⅝in); age 6 = 28.5 cm (11¼in).
9. **Ruffle trim length:** cut 2 same size pieces of ruffle trim according to size – for all sizes the trim fabric height needs to be 5cm (2in): age 2 = 32cm (12⅝in); age 3 = 33cm (13in); age 4 = 34cm (13⅜in); age 5 = 35cm (13¾in); age 6 = 36cm (14⅛in).
10. **Abbreviations used:** WS = wrong side, RS = right side, RST = right sides together, WST = wrong sides together, RSO = right sides out, WSO = wrong sides out.

Halter-Top Pattern Layout Diagrams

All yardage calculations include 11.3cm (⅛yd) buffer

Halter-Top
115cm (45in) fabric with/without nap
Age 2–3 = 0.5m (½yd)
Age 4–6 = 0.6m (⅝yd)

Halter-Top contrast trim fabric
92–115cm (36–45in) fabric with/without nap
Age 1–4 = 0.5m (½yd)
Age 5–6 = 0.6m (⅝yd)

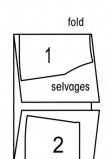

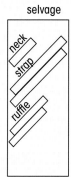

YOU WILL NEED

- Feature fabric for the dress – see pattern layout for amount
- Contrast fabric for the straps and trims – see Sewing Notes 5, 6 and 9
- Threads to match feature fabric and contrast fabric
- Elastic – see Sewing Notes 7 and 8
- Bodkin

Preparation

Cut all the fabric pieces as follows…

From the Happiness Halter-Top (top front, pattern piece No.1):
- 1 x on fold fabric

From the Happiness Halter-Top (top back, pattern piece No.2):
- 1 x on fold fabric

Also cut…
- Straps: 2 x pieces bias-cut contrast fabric 6cm (2⅜in) high – for length see Sewing Note 5
- Neckline binding: 1 x piece bias-cut contrast fabric 5cm (2in) – for length see Sewing Note 6
- Ruffle trim: 2 x pieces bias-cut contrast fabric 5cm (2in) – for length see Sewing Note 9
- Neckline elastic: 1 x piece 6mm (¼in) – for length see Sewing Note 7
- Back elastic 1 x piece 5mm (³⁄₁₆in) – for length see Sewing Note 8

Method

1 **Make the straps** – see Sewing Note 5. For both strap pieces fold the strips in half by bringing the long edges WST. Iron the fold, open the fabric out, fold in both long edges to the WS by 1cm (⅜in) and iron the folds. See **Photo 1**.

For straight straps, be accurate when folding in long edges by 1cm (⅜in).

2 **Make the neckline binding** – take the neckline binding fabric and fold it in the same way as the strap, but this time after unfolding the first set of folds you need to fold the long edges to the centre fold (not 1cm/⅜in as before). See Sewing Note 6.

3 **Make the ruffle trim** – see Sewing Note 9. The trim consists of two ruffle layers. In order to reduce bulk at the ruffle trim top edge the lower ruffle layer is stitched to the underside of the upper ruffle layer. Fold the ruffle trim strips in half by bringing the long edges WST, match all edges and iron the centre fold. Choose which ruffle trim you'd like as the underside layer and zigzag stitch along the raw top edge to prevent fraying. Unfold the other ruffle trim (the upper layer) and lay the zigzag-stitched trim down the upper layer long

edge centre RST. Pin as shown in **Photo 2**. Stitch 5mm (³⁄₁₆in) from the underside trim (zigzagged) top edge. Fold up the upper trim in half WST and admire your two-layer trim!

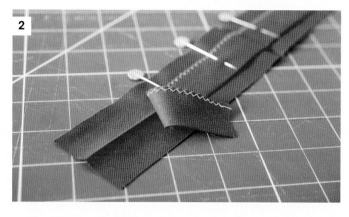

Lay the (folded) underside trim onto the unfolded (upper) trim RST and pin.

4 **Stitch the ruffle gathers** – stitch a double row of gathering stitches along the RS ruffle trim (upper layer ruffle) top edge (see Techniques: Gathering Stitches). Stitch the first row 2mm (⅛in) from the edge and the second row 6mm (¼in) in from the edge. See **Photo 3**.

As you stitch the second row, be careful to not stitch over the first row.

> TIP
> BE SURE TO STITCH NO MORE THAN 1CM (⅜IN) IN FROM THE EDGE, OR YOUR GATHERING STITCHES WILL SHOW ON THE FINISHED TOP.

5 **Stitch the ruffle trim to the neckline** – by finding and marking the ruffle centre top edge. Take the RSO ruffle and pin both short edges to the RS halter-top neckline. Do not pin through the gathering stitches. Pin the ruffle short edges 5mm (³⁄₁₆in) in from the halter-top sides. Match the ruffle and halter-top neckline centre points and pin. See **Photo 4**. Pull on the gather thread tails from both sides until the ruffle lies flat on the halter top neckline. Distribute the gathers evenly with your fingers. Pin and stitch the ruffles in place along the ruffle 5mm (³⁄₁₆in) down from the top edge. If you can, pull out and discard the gathering threads.

Pinning the ruffle to the neckline this way will help provide an even distribution of gathers when we pull on the bobbin thread.

6 **Stitch the neckline binding to the halter-top neckline** – unfold the neckline binding and find and mark the binding long edge centre. With the binding WSO, match the centre top edge points of the binding and halter-top neckline RS (with ruffle trim attached). There should be a 1cm (⅜in) clearance on either side of the binding. Match the raw top edges and stitch with a 5mm (³⁄₁₆in) seam. See **Photo 5**. Fold the binding back over the neckline (at the same time concealing the ruffle raw edge). The binding centre crease should butt up snugly with the neckline raw edge. Pin/clip the folded binding in place and stitch the binding to the RS halter-top neckline close to the binding bottom edge. Stitch on the RS.

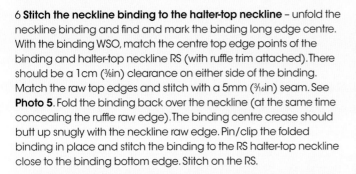

Ensure a 1cm (⅜in) clearance either side of the binding short edges and the side top edges of the halter-top front.

7 **Insert elastic into the neckline binding** – see Sewing Note 7. Use a bodkin to thread the elastic into the halter-top neckline WS binding (which doubles up as a casing). Leave 1cm (⅜in) of elastic sticking out of both casing ends. Stitch the elastic ends down through the casing 5mm (³⁄₁₆in) in from the casing side edges. Trim the elastic ends flush with the casing. See **Photo 6**.

Thread the elastic through at the WS of the fabric. When the elastic ends are securely stitched down, trim off the ends close to the casing edge.

8 **Stitch the opened straps to the halter-top front** – the straps are now stitched to the halter-top front curved side edges. Leaving the long edges folded, open one of the straps and place one of the halter-top front curved side edges into the unfolded binding. Align the halter-top side edge with the binding centre crease. Position and pin the opened binding to the halter-top side edge as shown in **Photo 7**.

3cm (1³⁄₁₆in)

Pin the opened strap to the halter-top 3cm (1³⁄₁₆in) down from the angled corner of the halter-top side.

9 **Finish stitching the straps to the top front** – fold in the strap short edge (at the top of the strap) to the WS by 1cm (⅜in) and iron the fold. Keeping the pins (from the previous step) in place, fold the opened strap back in half again (this will conceal the raw halter-top curved edge). Stitch the strap open edge shut 2mm (⅛in) from the strap edge. Stitch along the long open edge and then up the short side edge (at the top of the strap). See **Photo 8**. Repeat steps 8 and 9 for the other strap.

Stitch along the long and top short edge of the strap.

10 **Stitch a casing and insert elastic into the halter back** – this does the double-duty of finishing the raw top edge and creating a channel for the back elastic. Fold down the halter back top edge to the WS by 1cm (⅜in) iron the fold and repeat. Stitch the lower edge of the casing down 2mm (⅛in) from the edge. Insert elastic as described in Step 7. See **Photo 9**.

The elastic needs to reach the raw side edges of the back panel, to ensure it is stitched over in the next step.

11 **Stitch the halter back and front together** – bring the halter back and front side edges RST and pin. You will notice that the top left-hand and right-hand corners of the halter-top side edge overlap the halter-top front binding; also the binding bottom edge sticks out at the side seam – this is what we want. Pin and stitch on the halter WS. See **Photos 10** and **10.1**. Trim off the excess binding that sticks out of the side seam. Iron the seam open and zigzag stitch each seam layer to prevent fraying.

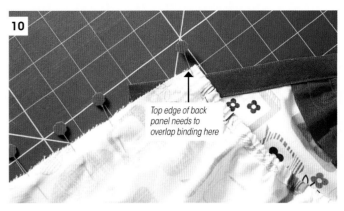

Top edge of back panel needs to overlap binding here

The very top edge of the back panel must overlap the binding so when you sew with a 1cm (⅜in) seam allowance the first stitch will hit the binding outer edge, allowing binding and back panel to flow into one another.

View of the finished top: in this close-up view you can see that the top edges of the front binding and the top edge of the halter-top appear to flow into each other.

12 **Stitch the hem** – fold up the hem raw edge by 1cm (⅜in) to the WS and iron the fold. Repeat, but this time fold up by 1.5cm (⅝in) to the WS. Stitch the hem down 2mm (⅛in) from the open edge of the hem to finish.

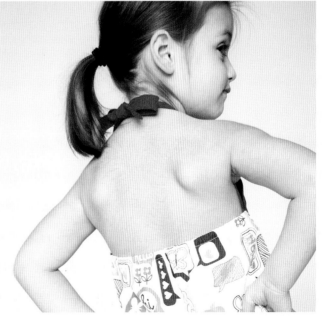

Dress

Perfect for parties or trips to sunny parks or beaches, this dress is as cute as it is versatile. Make one in an evening ready for your poppet to wear the next day. Handy pockets will store her party favours or seaside shells.

Sewing Notes

1. **Seam allowance:** 1cm (⅜in) unless otherwise stated. Seam allowance is included in the pattern pieces.
2. **Fabric recommendations:** lightweight cotton, tana lawn, quilt-weight cotton, needlecord cotton, chambray fabric.
3. **Pattern and fabric pieces:** the dress consists of: 6 x paper pattern pieces and 17 x fabric pattern pieces in total (including those from 'Also Cut' and elastic pieces).
4. **Waistband elastic length:** cut the waistband elastic according to size – for all sizes the elastic height needs to be 2cm (¾in). Feel free to lengthen or shorten the waist elastic: age 2 = 43cm (17in); age 3 = 45cm (17¾in); age 4 = 47cm (18½in); age 5 = 48.5cm (19⅛in); age 6 = 50cm (19¾in).
5. **Pocket trim length:** cut 2 same size pieces of pocket trim fabric according to size – for all sizes the trim fabric height needs to be 4cm (1⅝in): age 2 = 12cm (4¾in); age 3 = 12.5cm (4⅞in); age 4 = 13cm (5⅛in); age 5 = 13.5cm (5⁵⁄₁₆in); age 6 = 13.5cm (5⁵⁄₁₆in) (same as for age 5).
6. **Abbreviations used:** WS = wrong side, RS = right side, RST = right sides together, WST = wrong sides together, RSO = right sides out, WSO = wrong sides out.

YOU WILL NEED

- Feature fabric for dress – see pattern layout for fabric amount
- Contrast fabric for straps and trims – see pattern layout for amount
- Threads to match feature fabric and contrast fabric
- Elastic for waist 2cm (¾in) – for length see Sewing Note 4
- Elastic for neckline and back 5mm (¼in) – for length see Sewing Notes 7 and 8 of Halter-Top
- Bodkin

Preparation

Cut the fabric pieces as follows...

From Happiness Halter-Top (top front, pattern piece No.1):
- 1 x on fold fabric

From Happiness Halter-Top (top back, pattern piece No.2):
- 1 x on fold fabric

From Happiness Halter-Dress (skirt front, pattern piece No.3):
- 1 x on fold fabric

From Happiness Halter-Dress (skirt back, pattern piece No.4):
- 1 x on fold fabric

From Happiness Halter-Dress (skirt pocket lining, pattern piece No.5):
- 2 x fabric (cut 1 in mirror image)

From Happiness Halter-Dress (skirt pocket, pattern piece No.6):
- 2 x fabric (cut 1 in mirror image)

Also cut...

- Pocket binding 2 x pieces of bias-cut contrast fabric 4cm (1⅝in) x length according to age – see Sewing Note 5
- Waist elastic 1 x piece of 2cm (¾in) high x your calculation – see Sewing Note 4
- Cut all items noted in 'Also Cut' for the Halter-Top project

Dress Pattern Layout Diagrams

All yardage calculations include 11.3cm (⅛yd) buffer
Hashed lines = pattern pieces cut as mirror image

Dress
115cm (45in) fabric
with/without nap
Age 2–3 = 0.7m (¾yd)

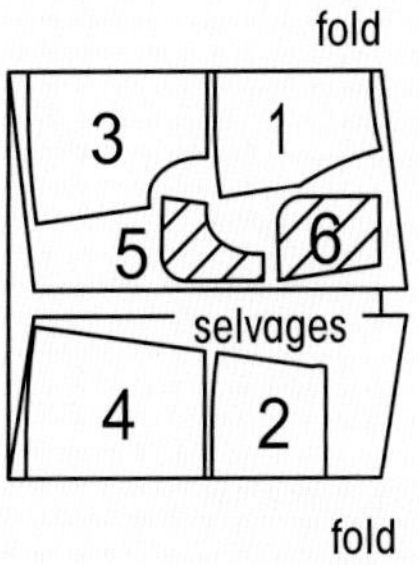

Dress
115cm (45in) fabric
with/without nap
Age 4 = 0.8m (⅞yd)
Age 5–6 = 0.9m (1yd)

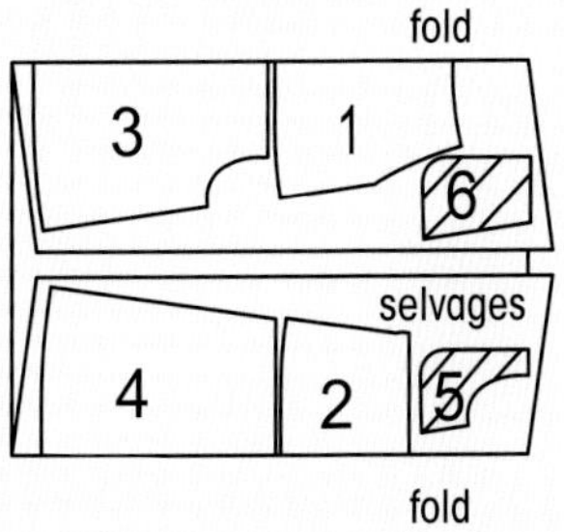

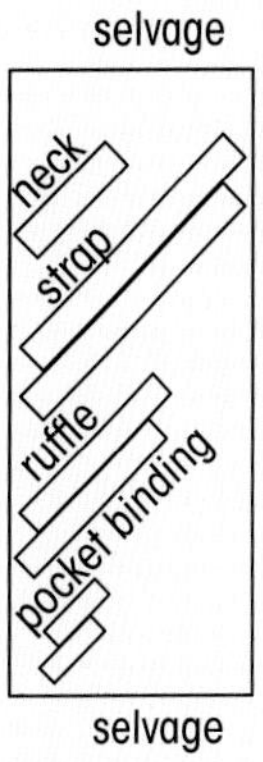

Dress contrast trim fabric
92–115cm (36–45in)
fabric with/without nap
Age 1–4 = 0.5m (½yd)
Age 5–6 = 0.6m (⅝yd)

Method

1 **Make the halter-top** – following Steps 1–11 of the Halter-Top project.

2 **Make the pocket binding** – take one of the pocket binding fabric pieces, fold it in half by bringing the long edges WST. Iron the centre fold, open out and fold the long edges to the centre crease and iron. Repeat with the other binding piece. Set aside.

3 **Position the pocket binding** – bring the skirt front fabric piece (or shorts/pants front fabric, if making) and pocket lining pieces WST. Carefully match the pocket curve, side and top edges of both pieces. Bind the two fabric pieces together at the pocket curve. Position the pocket binding 1cm (⅜in) down from the pocket curve top edge. Clip/pin the binding in place and stitch 2mm (⅛in) from the binding open edge. See **Photo 1**. Repeat with the other side of the skirt and pocket lining piece.

6 **Stitch the skirt** – bring the skirt fabric pieces RST, match both side edges, and pin and stitch each side edge with a 1cm (⅜in) seam. Iron the seams open and zigzag stitch both seam layers to prevent fraying.

7 **Stitch the skirt hem** – fold up the bottom hem raw edge by 1cm (⅜in) to the WS and iron the fold. Repeat, but this time fold up by 1.5cm (⅝in) to the WS. Stitch the hem down 2mm (⅛in) from the first folded edge of the hem.

8 **Stitch the skirt to the halter-top** – insert the skirt RSO into the halter-top WSO so that the skirt top edge and the halter bottom RS edges are matched. Match the side seams of both. See **Photo 3**. Pin and stitch with a 2.5cm (1in) seam (I'll now refer to this seam as the 'waistband'). Neatly zigzag stitch the waistband raw edge. If necessary trim any straggly bits from the seam edge.

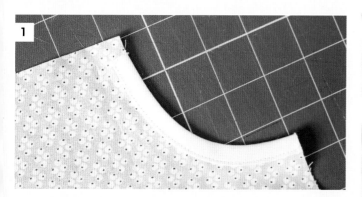

Stitch the binding 1cm (⅜in) down from the pocket curved top edge, to reduce bulk at the waistband seam at a later stage.

Place the skirt into the halter top – the RS of both should now be touching each other.

4 **Position and pin the pocket** – with the skirt front WSO, bring the pocket and pocket lining pieces RST. Carefully match all edges and pin all around the inner side and bottom edges.

5 **Complete the pocket construction** – stitch the pocket to the pocket lining. As you sew the pocket pieces together ensure that you keep the skirt front fabric tucked out of the way of your needle. Then, to prevent fraying, zigzag stitch the curved seam. In preparation for the next step, pin the pocket outer side seam to the skirt front side seam. See **Photo 2**. Repeat Steps 4 and 5 for the other pocket.

Stitch the pocket and pocket lining together and zigzag stitch the pocket raw edges.

9 **Make a casing for the elastic on the waistband** – turn the skirt WSO (so entire garment is WSO). Push the waistband up so it's lying flat on the halter-top WS. Iron the waistband in place and pin onto the halter-top. See **Photo 4**. Stitch the waistband to the halter-top leaving a gap of 7.5cm (3in) in the centre waistband back (for the elastic). Stitch 3mm (⅛in) from the waistband zigzagged edge. Take your time to sew in a straight line as these stitches will be visible on the finished garment. Now the waistband has been stitched to the halter-top I'll refer the waistband as the 'casing'.

10 **Insert the elastic into the casing** – attach your bodkin to your pre-measured waistband elastic (see Sewing Note 4) and thread it into the casing gap. Thread the elastic all around the casing until you are holding both elastic ends in your fingers. Overlap the elastic ends by 1.3cm (½in), pin and stitch together. See **Photo 5**. Allow the elastic to ping back into the casing. Stitch the waistband gap shut as described in Step 9.

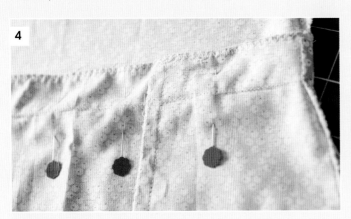

Fold the waistband up onto the halter-top WS and pin in place

Overlap the elastic ends by 1.3cm (1³⁄₁₆in), pin and stitch together with two lines of stitches.

Playsuit

This playsuit is sweet and a little cheeky. Cute details such as pockets, puffy legs and yummy ruffle trim provide many styling options. Have fun mixing and matching your favourite fabric prints and/or solids to make coordinated or hotchpotch playsuits that will brighten up any girl's wardrobe.

Sewing Notes

1. Seam allowance: 1cm (⅜in) unless otherwise stated. Seam allowance is included in the pattern pieces.
2. Fabric recommendations: – lightweight cotton, tana lawn, quilt-weight cotton, needlecord cotton, chambray fabric.
3. Pattern pieces: the playsuit is made of: 6 x paper pattern pieces and 21 x fabric pattern pieces in total (including those from 'Also Cut').
4. Shorts (pants) length: feel free to shorten/lengthen the shorts. Simply decide on your chosen leg length and add on/subtract from the shorts front and back pattern pieces as necessary. Be sure to follow the side edges angles of the shorts front and back pattern pieces.
5. Leg bottom (cuff) fabric width: the leg cuff width depends on the amount of desired puffiness and the width of your poppet's leg. In preparation for Step 8, measure around her leg just above her knee. If you have modified the leg length pattern, measure around her leg at the point where the legs will end and add on a further 5cm (2in) for wiggle-room and seam allowance. The leg cuff fabric needs to be 9cm (3½in) high. Or you can follow my leg cuff fabric width recommendations as follows: cut two same size pieces of bias-cut fabric for the leg bottoms (cuffs) according to size – for all sizes the fabric height needs to be 9cm (3½in): age 2 = 34.5cm (13⅝in); age 3 = 35cm (13¾in); age 4 = 35.5cm (14in); age 5 = 36cm (14⅛in); age 6 = 37cm (14⅝in).
6. Abbreviations used: WS = wrong side, RS = right side, RST = right sides together, WST = wrong sides together, RSO = right sides out, WSO = wrong sides out.

YOU WILL NEED

- Feature fabric for playsuit – see pattern layout for fabric amount
- Contrast fabric for straps and trims – see pattern layout for amount
- Threads to match feature fabric and contrast fabric
- Elastic for waist 2cm (¾in) – for length see Sewing Note 4 of Dress project
- Bodkin

Preparation

Cut the fabric pieces as follows…
From Happiness Halter-Top (top front, pattern piece No.1):
- 1x on fold fabric

From Happiness Halter-Top (top back, pattern piece No.2):
- 1 x on fold fabric

From Happiness Halter Playsuit (shorts/pants back, pattern piece No.8):
- 2 x fabric (cut 1 in mirror image)

From Happiness Halter Playsuit (shorts/pants front, pattern piece No.7):
- 2 x fabric (cut 1 in mirror image)

From Happiness Halter Playsuit (shorts/pants pocket, pattern piece No.10):
- 2 x fabric (cut 1 in mirror image)

From Happiness Halter Playsuit (shorts/pants pocket lining, pattern piece No.9):
- 2 x fabric (cut 1 in mirror image)

Also cut…

- Leg cuffs: 2 pieces of feature fabric 9cm (3½in) (length is variable – see Sewing Note 5)
- Pocket binding 2 x pieces of contrast fabric 4cm (1⅝in) – see Sewing Note 5 of Dress project
- Waist elastic 1 x piece of 2cm (¾in) (length is variable – see Sewing Note 4 of Dress project)
- See 'Also Cut' in Dress project and cut all pieces in that section

Playsuit Pattern Layout Diagrams

All yardage calculations include 11.3cm (⅛yd) buffer
Hashed lines = pattern pieces cut as mirror image

Playsuit
115cm (45in) fabric with/without nap
Age 3 = 0.8m (⅞yd)
Age 4–5 = 0.9m (1yd)
Age 6 = 1m (1⅛yd)

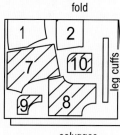

Playsuit
115cm (45in) fabric with/without nap
Age 2 = 0.7m (¾yd)

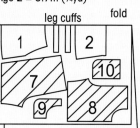

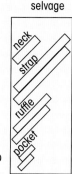

Playsuit contrast trim fabric
92–115cm (36–45in) fabric with/without nap
Age 1–4 = 0.5m (½yd)
Age 5–6 = 0.6m (⅝yd)

Method

1 **Make the halter-top** – following Steps 1–11 of the Halter-Top project.

2 **Cut the leg cuffs** – cut the fabric to your cuff width measurement (see Sewing Note 5).

3 **Fold the leg cuff** – for both cuff pieces fold the strips in half by bringing the long edges WST and iron the fold. Open the fabric out, fold in both long edges to the WS by 1cm (⅜in) and iron the folds. See **Photo 1**. Stitch the short edges of the leg cuffs RST. Trim the seam corners and iron the seams open. Repeat for other leg cuff.

Be accurate when folding in the long edges by 1cm (⅜in) for a professional-looking leg cuff and to make attaching them easier.

4 **Make the pockets** – to trim and make the pockets follow Steps 2–5 of the Dress project.

5 **Stitch the shorts (pants) front panels** – bring the two shorts front panels RST and match all edges. Pin and stitch together all along the curved edge. Iron the seam open and prevent fraying by zigzag stitching each seam layer. See **Photo 2**.

Stitch the short front panels RST along the curved edge.

6 **Stitch the shorts (pants) back panels** – bring the two shorts back fabric panels RST, match all edges, pin and stitch together all along the curved edge. Iron the seam open and prevent fraying by zigzag stitching each seam layer.

7 **Stitch the shorts front and back inseam** – bring the shorts front and back pieces RST. Take your time to neatly match the shorts front and back curved seams and inseam raw edges. Pin and stitch together along the shorts inseam (see Tip). Iron the seam open and prevent fraying by zigzag stitching each seam layer. See **Photo 3**.

For a neat X at the crotch, carefully match inseams and curved seams.

> **TIP**
> IN CASE YOU WERE WONDERING, THE 'INSEAM' IS
> THE SEAM THAT BEGINS AT THE CROTCH AND ENDS AT THE BOTTOM EDGE
> OF THE LEG OF THE TROUSERS/PANTS LEG.

8 **Gather the leg bottoms** – the leg bottoms are gathered according to your leg cuff size (see Sewing Note 5). You will need to gather the leg bottoms to the same measurement as your leg cuff fabric. For example, if your leg cuff fabric was 35cm (13¾in) you will need to gather the leg bottoms to 35cm (13¾in). Open out one of the legs and sew two lines of gathering stitches on the bottom edge – sew the first row 2mm (⅛in) from the edge and the second row 6mm (¼in) in from the edge. Begin (and end) your gathering stitches 1.5cm (⅝in) in from the shorts (pants) side and inseam edges. Pull on the bobbin thread until you reach the desired leg bottom width. When satisfied, stitch the gathers in place by sewing a line of stitches just below the gathering stitches. If you can, pull and discard the gathering threads from the fabric. See **Photo 4**.

Gather the leg bottoms as desired, according to your sizes of leg cuff fabric width. Distribute the gathers evenly and then stitch in place.

9 **Stitch the shorts (pants) sides** – with the shorts WSO carefully match the shorts front and back side edges, pin and stitch both sides. Iron the seams open and prevent fraying by zigzag stitching each seam layer.

10 **Stitch the leg cuff to the bottom leg** – we are now going to bind the leg bottom edges with the leg cuffs. Slip one of the leg cuffs around a leg bottom edge RST. Ensure the cuff seam is in line with the leg inseam. Match the raw edges, pin and stitch all around the leg bottom. See **Photo 5**. Neatly fold the leg cuff back on the cuff folds, smooth down any bumps, pin the folds in place and stitch all around 2mm (⅛in) from the cuff open edge. See **Photo 5.1**. Repeat Steps 8–10 for the other leg and leg cuff.

5

If you are unable to remove the gathering stitches, move stray threads towards the leg bottom edge, so they won't show on the finished playsuit.

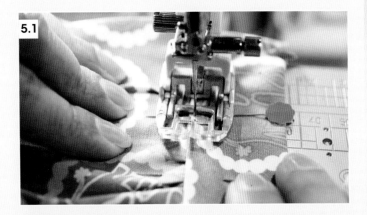

5.1

Stitch the leg cuff in place all around the leg bottom.

11 **Attach the shorts (pants) to the halter-top** – to attach the shorts to the top and finish off, follow Steps 8–10 of the Dress project. The method is the same for both the shorts and dress.

General Techniques

This section describes the general techniques used to make the garments.

Preparation and Cutting Tips

- It's wise to pre-wash fabrics before using them, because the first wash can cause shrinkage. To minimize fraying in the wash, snip off the fabric selvedge corners or zigzag stitch the fabric's cut edges – see Techniques: Zigzag Stitching.
- Thoroughly iron your fabrics before pattern cutting.
- Iron your paper patterns before using.
- Change machine needles regularly – ideally with each new project.
- Use a pressing cloth when ironing your garments, to protect them from iron scorch/dirt/water/shine marks.
- Always cut on a flat, cleared surface.
- Always use *sharp* rotary cutters and scissors. Dull blades cause accidents from having to exert too much effort into cutting, which leads to slipping.
- Carefully follow grain lines to ensure that fabric designs do not appear uneven (see Understanding Patterns).

Understanding Patterns

Besides the pattern shape, there is a variety of other information on pattern pieces, as shown in the diagram here.

- **Seam allowance** – this is the distance between the edge of the fabric piece(s) and the sewing machine needle. So, if a pattern indicates a seam allowance of 1cm (⅜in), you need to sew your stitches 1cm (⅜in) in from the edge of the fabric. The pattern instructions should always state the seam allowance size and whether or not it has been included in the pattern.
- **Grain lines** – double-pointed arrows that help you align the pattern piece with the straight grain of the fabric. The top arrow points to the top edge of the fabric and the bottom arrow to the bottom edge. The straight grain of the fabric runs parallel to the selvedge (the non-fraying edge, which often has the company and fabric name printed on it).
- **Fold lines** – when a pattern piece says 'place on fold' you need to fold your fabric wrong sides together and place the edge of the pattern piece onto the fabric fold. The resulting cut fabric piece will be double the size.
- **Notches** – lines that appear on the pattern piece outline. They help you to match up seams and fabric edges accurately. Pattern pieces that need joining up will have corresponding notches. Transfer pattern notches to your fabric pieces using a disappearing marker or make small nicks with sharp scissors.
- **Other pattern markings** – button placements and so on, need to be traced onto your patterns and then transferred to your fabric pieces.

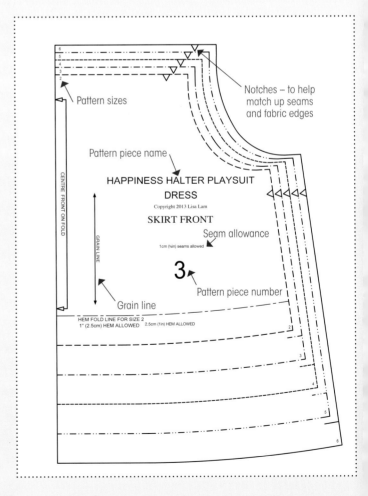

Gathering Stitches

Gathering stitches are used when you want to insert gathers into your fabric. You can set your machine to sew a long and loose stitch, which means you can easily pull on the bobbin threads to gather up your fabric. Using a thicker thread can also help. The results look great and it's very simple and satisfying to do.

1 **Set up your sewing machine** – set your machine to the longest straight/normal stitch and set your bobbin thread to tension #1. These settings will provide a bobbin thread that is loose enough for you to pull easily so you can 'pucker up'/gather your fabric.

2 **Sew the gathering stitches** – leaving long thread tails at both ends, stitch along the item that you want to gather. Do not sew securing stitches at either end of your gathering stiches. Stitch a double row of gathering stitches (see Tip). Your pattern should state the location and how far apart the two rows of gathering stitches should be sewn. See **Photo 1**.

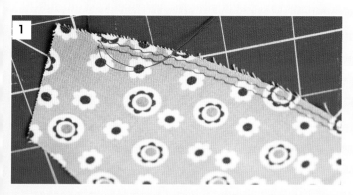

When you stitch the second row of gathering stitches, be careful not to stitch over the first row.

TIP

A DOUBLE ROW OF GATHERING STITCHES IS MORE STABLE THAN A SINGLE ROW BECAUSE IT IS LESS LIKELY TO UNRAVEL (PING BACK) AFTER YOU HAVE GATHERED YOUR FABRIC. HOWEVER YOU SEW YOUR GATHERING STITCHES, BE SURE TO STITCH *INSIDE* YOUR SEAM ALLOWANCE OR YOUR GATHERING STITCHES WILL SHOW ON THE FINISHED GARMENT.

3 **Reset your machine** – remember to reset your stitch length and bobbin tension before you continue sewing.

4 **Pulling up and securing the gathers** – pull up the gathering threads to the required width. Pin the gathers to secure them in position and then machine straight stitch in place.

5 **Discarding the gathering stitches** – if possible, try to remove the gathering stitches by completely pulling out the bobbin thread. The top thread will also come away and you can discard both threads. As there are occasions where you need to stitch over the gathering stitches it won't always be possible to remove them. If gathering stitches are sewn inside the seam allowance they will not show on the finished garment.

Zigzag Stitching

When sewing it's important to neaten the seam raw edges, as this will help prevent fraying, thus prolonging the life of your garment. Using a zigzag stitch on the seam edges is a quick and effective way to neaten the seams on most types of fabric.

1 **Set your sewing machine** – set your machine to zigzag stitch and fit your zigzag foot.

2 **Find the stitch width and length** – for this it's best to experiment on a fabric scrap (doubled over if you are stitching two layers or single layer if you are sewing single layer). I find that a stitch length of 2.5 and a stitch width of 5.5 works well for me, but experiment to find out what works best for your machine and fabric. See **Photo 1**.

This is how a nice and even zigzagged hem should look. The stitch width is wide enough to stitch over the raw edge and back into the seam and the length is long enough to cover the seam and not so short it creates bumps in the seam.

3 **Stitch your seam** – align your fabric seam edge with the machine foot centre and sew zigzag stitch over the seam edge. You will notice that as the needle sweeps to the right the needle will pass over the fabric and totally miss it. What is actually happening is that the right-hand pass of the needle wraps a thread over the seam edge. As the needle sweeps to the left, the needle pierces through the fabric (anchoring the stitch in the fabric).

Suppliers

UK

U-Handbag
www.u-handbag.com
One-stop shop for bag making supplies, sewing notions, patterns and kits with worldwide delivery

Backstitch
Tel: 01749 675 272
www.backstitch.co.uk
Pretty fabrics, sewing patterns and a craft blog

Clover
Tel: 0081 (06) 6978-2220
www.clover-mfg.com/euro/index/english.html
For a huge range of haberdashery, quilting supplies and equipment

The Cotton Patch
Tel: 0121 702 2840
www.cottonpatch.co.uk
For patchwork and quilting fabrics, books, wadding, notions and haberdashery

Eclectic Maker
Tel: 0845 862 5552
www.eclecticmaker.co.uk/
Lovely fabrics and haberdashery

Fabrics Galore
www.fabricsgalore.co.uk/
For a selection of Liberty fabrics at reduced prices

Janome
Tel: 0161 666 6011
www.janome.co.uk
I've always been a Janome girl. I created these patterns on a Janome MemoryCraft 8900 QCP and my machine and I had a great time in the process!

Plush Addict
Tel: 0845 519 4422
www.plushaddict.co.uk
For a massive choice of fabrics including the entire Kona Solids range – amazing!

The Village Haberdashery
Tel: 0207 794 5635
www.thevillagehaberdashery.co.uk/
Great range of fabric and trims

USA

Amy Butler
Tel: 740-587-2841
www.amybutlerdesign.com
One of my favourite fabric designers (with a very inspirational website)

fabric.com
Tel: 770-792-8590
www.fabric.com
Huge selection of fabrics, patterns and sewing machines

Hawthorne Threads
Tel: 800-965-8746
www.hawthornethreads.com/
Lovely fabric shop with helpful ideas for matching fabrics

Quilt Home
www.quilthome.com/
Huge range of fabrics

Westminster Fibers
Tel: 866-907-3305
www.westminsterfibers.com/fabric.html
Manufacturers of some of my favourite quilting fabrics including Amy Butler and Free Spirit

A DAVID & CHARLES BOOK
© F&W Media International, Ltd 2014
David & Charles is an imprint of F&W Media International, Ltd
Brunel House, Forde Close, Newton Abbot, TQ12 4PU, UK

F&W Media International, Ltd is a subsidiary of F+W Media, Inc
10151 Carver Road, Suite #200, Blue Ash, OH 45242, USA

Text and Designs © Lisa Lam 2014
Layout and Photography © F&W Media International, Ltd 2014.
The author consents to the sale of garments made using this pattern on the condition that the author is credited as the designer in all product descriptions. Consent does not extend to factory manufacture or mass production. First published in the UK and USA in 2014.

Lisa Lam has asserted her right to be identified as author of this work in accordance with the Copyright, Designs and Patents Act, 1988.

The author and publisher have made every effort to ensure that all the instructions in the book are accurate and safe, and therefore cannot accept liability for any resulting injury, damage or loss to persons or property, however it may arise.

Names of manufacturers and product ranges are provided for the information of readers, with no intention to infringe copyright or trademarks.

A catalogue record for this book is available from the British Library.
ISBN-13: 978-1-4463-0446-4 paperback
ISBN-10: 1-4463-0446-9 paperback

Printed in China by RR Donnelley

10 9 8 7 6 5 4 3 2 1

Acquisitions Editor: Sarah Callard
Desk Editor: Harriet Butt
Project Editor: Lin Clements
Pattern Checker: Debora Davis
Designer: Charly Bailey
Photographer: Jack Kirby
Production: Bev Richardson

F+W Media publishes high quality books on a wide range of subjects. For more great book ideas visit: www.stitchcraftcreate.co.uk

Fabrics used:
All feature fabrics are by Westminster Fibers or Free Spirit. All solids are Kona Solids.

Halter-Top (main photo) feature fabric = Moxie, Chatterbox, sky PWEM045; Contrast fabric = Kona Water.
Halter-Top (instructions) feature fabric = Moxie, Chatterbox, tangerine PWEM045; Contrast fabric = Kona Pomegrante.
Dress (main photo) feature fabric Moxie, Chatterbox, sky PWEM047; Contrast fabric = Kona Snow.
Dress (instructions) feature fabric Florence, Four Dots, malachite PWDS050; Contrast fabric = Kona Snow.
Playsuit (main photo) feature fabric Circa, Lindsey, green PWJ071; Contrast fabric = Kona Delf.
Playsuit (instructions) Bridgette Lane, Bouncing Elephants, honey tea PWVW060; Contrast fabric = Kona Snow.

Sizing Charts

Happiness Halter-Top
Width of hem x height (neck to hem)
Age 2 = 32cm x 26cm (12½ x 10¼in)
Age 3 = 34cm x 27.3cm (13⅜ x 10¾in)
Age 4 = 35cm x 28.5cm (13¾ x 11¼in)
Age 5 = 37cm x 29.8cm (14½ x 11¾in)
Age 6 = 38cm x 31.1cm (15 x 12¼in)

Happiness Dress/Playsuit
Max width (at waist)
Age 2 = 35cm (13¾in)
Age 3 = 36cm (14⅛in)
Age 4 = 38cm (15in)
Age 5 = 39cm (15⅜in)
Age 6 = 41cm (16⅛in)

Happiness Dress
Height (neckline to hem)
Age 2 = 39cm (15⅜in)
Age 3 = 47cm (18½in)
Age 4 = 51cm (20in)
Age 5 = 51cm (22½in)
Age 6 = 62.5cm (24⅝in)

Happiness Playsuit
Height (neckline to hem)
Age 2 = 51.5cm (20¼in)
Age 3 = 55.5cm (21⅞in)
Age 4 = 59cm (23¼in)
Age 5 = 62.5cm (25¾in)
Age 6 = 68cm (26¾in)